Ediciones Polígrafa

SANAA: SEJIMA & NISHIZAWA

NEW MUSEUM

NEW YORK

Photographic essay by Iwan Baan

© of this edition: Ediciones Polígrafa, Barcelona, 2010
Balmes, 54. 08007 Barcelona (Spain)
www.edicionespoligrafa.com

© of the photographs, texts, and translations: the authors

Photographic credits: Dean Kaufman (pp. 21, 26-28),
Iwan Baan (cover, pp. 7, 9, 32-71)

Concept of the Collection: Francisco Rei
Coordination: Marcela Carrasquilla
Copy Editor: Richard G. Gallin
Design: mot (www.motstudio.com)
Page layout: Estudi Polígrafa / Carlos J. Santos
Color separation: Estudi Polígrafa / Annel Biu
Printing and binding: Novoprint, Barcelona (Spain)

Available in USA and Canada through
D.A.P./Distributed Art Publishers
155 Sixth Avenue, 2nd Floor, New York, N.Y. 10013
Tel. (212) 627-1999; Fax: (212) 627-9484

ISBN: 978-84-343-1244-9
Dep. legal: B. 41015 - 2010

Backcover: Excerpt of interview with Kazuyo Sejima and
Ryue Nishizawa. Firts published in Shift: SANAA and the
New Museum, Lars Müller Publishers, 2008, p. 26.

CONTENTS

Aerial view of the
New Museum and the
surrounding area in New
York City, United States
Photo: Iwan Baan

Detail of the aluminum mesh
of the New Museum at dusk
Photo: Iwan Baan

The New Museum of Contemporary Art was founded thirty-three years ago with a vision to show new art and new ideas when few museums were doing so. It was the brainchild of Marcia Tucker, a curator with no financial resources or collection of her own whose daring vision that an institution like this should exist – indeed, *needed* to exist in New York – propelled the museum forward.

The 1970s were a time of idealistic alternatives that revolutionized culture through grassroots efforts. All the profound social and political transformations of the 1960s began to be expressed in new kinds of cultural organizations. Alternative spaces proliferated in the 1970s as a new species of art organization that persists to this day as a critical part of the cultural food chain. The New Museum began as just such an organization – with big ambitions built into its paradoxical name. In its first year the New Museum operated only a small office with a staff of three and soon migrated to a gallery space at the New School for Social Research, before moving again in 1983 to a storefront loft space on Broadway in SoHo. An important part of Tucker's vision was to embrace the innovative and inquisitive spirit of contemporary art as a means of reenvisioning the institution of the museum. She believed that there was a posture of inquiry that certain artists had that museums could learn from. This double commitment not only to showcase but also to learn from the work of living artists remains an essential part of the New Museum's guiding mission.

In 1999 when I joined the museum as Director, the New Museum was at a crossroads. Marcia Tucker had stepped down to retire, and many of the innovations the New Museum had pioneered had been absorbed by mainstream institutions. The art world had also changed substantially, and old polarities of margin versus mainstream no longer held strong. Most importantly, contemporary art had become ubiquitous, popular with mainstream audiences, and embraced by institutions large and small. It was time to reinvent again. The New Museum desperately needed better gallery space, a higher public profile, and a broader visitorship – an essential part of its original mission, to bring leading-edge contemporary art to wider audiences. And so the decision was made to take the big step – to build our first freestanding building, doubling our size. Naturally this decision was also charged with the challenge of growing while remaining true to the mission and core values of the museum, and continuing to innovate.

In 2000 the search for a site began. We scoured the city, from the Battery to Harlem, considered Brooklyn and Queens, and negotiated sites in Chelsea and the Meat Market. Then 9/11 happened, and we renewed our commitment to Downtown, the center of the creative community for decades and the neighborhood we had always been part of. Rather than setting us back or slowing us down, that tragic event gave us the strong resolve to move forward in a bold, confident way. We found several potential sites (on Bond Street, on Lafayette Street, and on the Bowery), but the one that the Board responded unanimously to was a nondescript parking lot on the Bowery at the head of Prince Street, visible down Prince Street from the corner of Prince and Broadway.

The Bowery was so close and yet so far from our former home on Broadway. It was still a no-man's-land, stigmatized and neglected while all around it things were changing and springing to life. Could we help to transform this storied street? It was a street with such a rich history, and one whose charms artists had recognized for decades: a broad boulevard with lots of light, accessible by many subway lines, surrounded by heterogeneous communities.

We wanted a building that was striking and surprising, one that would elicit curiosity and would reflect our identity through its form. We also wanted a building made of common industrial materials in keeping with the Bowery neighborhood, a building that would be both scrappy and stylish. One of the key elements of our program was to test the possibility of building outstanding architecture for a reasonable per-square-foot cost, using low-cost materials and standard modular components. This was aligned with our values (and our limited resources). Gigantism would not be our key to success. Rather, right sizing and making an impact at a smaller scale through independent thinking, a good process, and a degree of artistic freedom were paramount.

We also knew that we could be a great client and make a contribution to the architecture of the city. In keeping with our mission to show new art, often giving artists their first museum exposure, we resolved to work with an architectural firm that was not yet recognized here and give them the opportunity to build their first building in New York. Consistent with our global mission, we opened our search to firms from around the world – from Asia, Europe, and South America, as well as the United States.

We considered more than forty-five firms through a Request for Qualifications process and eventually narrowed those down to five finalists whom we invited to participate in a closed design competition in late 2002. The five short-listed choices were Reiser + Umemoto, RUR Architecture PC, New York; Abalos & Herreros, Madrid; Gigon/Guyer, Zurich; Adjaye/Associates, London; and Kazuyo Sejima + Ryue Nishizawa/SANAA, Tokyo. (The SAANA stands for Sejima and Nishizawa and Associates.) Each proposed magnificent buildings, but SANAA's scheme was selected for best bringing the site, the New Museum's mission, and the program into alignment through their design. Their stunning solution to the zoning envelope was a stacked set of rectangular boxes shifted off a central core. They did not maximize the allowable square footage, but instead created a shifting and open form – a dynamic sculptural solution, which perfectly reflected both the Museum's mission and the changing nature of contemporary art. Where the boxes shifted, skylights let light in, providing a remarkable lightness and openness to the whole shifting mass.

SANAA worked in the service of the New Museum's vision, but they also heightened it. Their approach was informed and driven by the program we established. Rather than impose a house style, they listened to us and analyzed the program to come up with an optimal solution. SANAA also delivered architecture that would best serve the art and not get in the way or compete with it. Their deceptively simple design is highly calibrated and shows art to its best advantage without intruding on it. We believed from the start that if the architecture could achieve this, it would in itself be innovative.

There is an immediate element of surprise when you first see the building. One of the most surprising things is its transparency. You see art and people from the first instant through the floor-to-ceiling glass storefront. You see the back-of-house machinations through the transparent glass freight entrance.

Then in a final flourish of alchemy arrived at during the design development phase, SANAA clad the entire building in an expanded aluminum mesh that optically dematerializes the building and turns the entire structure into a play of light and reflection. The mesh is constantly changing as the light changes with the weather, the time of day, and the seasons. The whole skin becomes a moving animated surface, and the volume of the building is softened and made ethereal, receding into the landscape from many vantage points.

Since December 2007, more than a million people have passed through the doors of our new home, and we have become a major cultural destination. Our visitors come from all over the world, and international tourists account for 40 percent of our audience. On the Bowery, we have mounted more than forty-three exhibitions with work by 245 artists from fifty countries in a varied program of one-artist shows, timely thematic presentations, cross-institutional collaborations, and signature initiatives. We have also presented over two hundred public programs in our new theater and are also a neighborhood anchor — our lobby, open to the public free of charge, buzzes with activity; sixty new art galleries have opened around us, and new restaurants and retail operations flock to the area.

In the past decade, the cultural landscape has been driven by unrelenting growth. SANAA's efficient ability to balance design vision and the client's program resulted in an instant landmark destination for contemporary art in a city that is a world capital of art. In May 2010 Kazuyo Sejima and Ryue Nishizawa were awarded the Pritzker Architecture Prize for their body of work with a special recognition of the New Museum. Their brilliant design announces a museum that is open, fearless, and alive: a thing of beauty, and also an unpredictable and unstable place of curiosity, discovery, and exploration.

Lisa Phillips
Toby Devan Lewis Director
New Museum of Contemporary Art

"THE ARTWORK IS
NEVER AN ADDED
DIFFICULTY"

Conversation with
Kazuyo Sejima and Ryue
Nishizawa

However paradoxical it might seem, the New Museum, set up more than three decades ago by Marcia Tucker, never until now had a building of its own to host the busy, demanding program pursued over the years.

Toward the end of 2002, five architecture offices were invited to submit proposals to build a permanent home for the museum. The competition concluded months later with the award of the project to SANAA, an office consisting of Kazuyo Sejima (b. 1956) and Ryue Nishizawa (b. 1966). The dialogue between the architects and Lisa Phillips, director of the New Museum, is an example of the interaction and synergies that can be established when "formalizing" a program centered on contemporaneity and experimentation. As Kazuyo Sejima puts it: "The New Museum has always been at the forefront of innovation and experimentation, so I think it's appropriate and consistent with the institution's identity. The expectations are very different if you're designing a special contemporary art space or a downtown office block, so you have to take advantage of every aspect of the program's potential. The obvious problem is that if the building is tall and the floors simply replicate a typical plan, the instinctive reaction is "oh, this is an office building," and only later you might discover there's a gallery inside. The fundamental objective was to avoid that trap. I feel the New Museum is not a normal museum — it's something in between a gallery and an event space. It is experimental, and its architectural identity must also be experimental. I feel, and I hope other people feel, that this building is suited to the museum's character."

The Japanese architects also demonstrated the wealth of their concepts; at that time they were busy constructing the Glass Pavilion at the Toldeo Museum of Art in Toledo, Ohio, which is another of their key works. Ryue Nishizawa reveals the differences between the two buildings: "Our spatial strategy for the New Museum was very different from the one adopted for the Glass Museum in Toledo. In Toledo the exhibition spaces are to some extent neutral, and given the transparency of the walls they are all constantly interconnected or somehow relating to one another. What emerged from our conversations with the director and staff of the New Museum was a desire to create a more complex narrative, in which the spatial experience and the proportions of the galleries could change from floor to floor, and in which there would be surprises like the narrow stairway and the 'shaft' exhibition space."

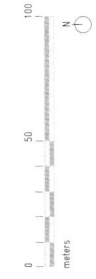

Question._ The beginning of a new century has historically been marked by the dynamics of the change it has embraced, and in this regard the twenty-first century is no exception. Museums, which traditionally have stored the relics of our culture, now seem to want to capture the present, if not to steal a march on the future. Under what conceptual premises does one design an art museum of the twenty-first century, when this has only just begun?

Kazuyo Sejima and Ryue Nishzawa._ We design museums that concern themselves with the future by thinking about openness, which manifests itself as room for new possibilities as well as simple physical connection beyond and through its walls.

As distinct from other typologies, the architectural conception of a museum must take into account the critical presence of the artwork. Do you regard this dialectical confrontation between the two practices as an added difficulty?

The artwork is never an added difficulty. We try to allow the art its own context, one that is not necessarily related to our work.

What has been your approach to art?

Some art touches us and makes us feel something that we did not feel before. Architecture can do the same for us. On the level of the body it can often be the same thing.

And in the field of architecture, what have been your referents?

There are too many references to name. We love many things.

Are we correct in appreciating the ideas of *container*, associated with storage — a pile of boxes — and *shift* as key ones for the New Museum?

We are perhaps most interested in the opening that comes from the shift. The pile is meant to feel natural, but it has a logic that relates to the openings produced by the shifts. The openings and platforms, where the Bowery comes in, attract us.

GALLERY

CAFE

SHOP

LOBBY

HOLDING

1st Floor

MECHANICAL

CLEAN ROOM

THEATER

STORAGE

STORAGE

Basement Floor

GALLERY

3rd Floor

GALLERY

2nd Floor

6th Floor

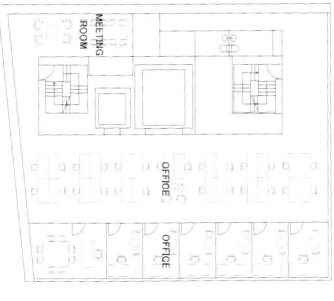

MEETING ROOM

OFFICE

OFFICE

4th Floor

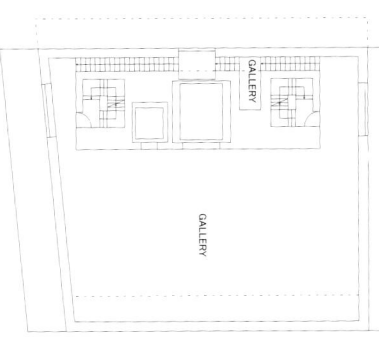

GALLERY

GALLERY

7th Floor

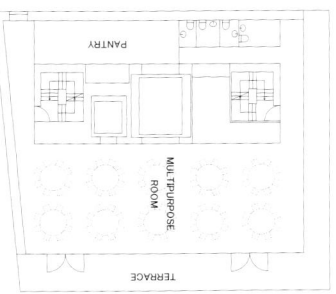

PANTRY

MULTIPURPOSE ROOM

TERRACE

5th Floor

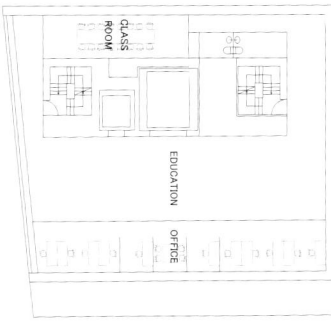

CLASS ROOM

EDUCATION

OFFICE

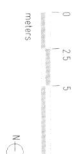
meters

0
2.5
5
10

N

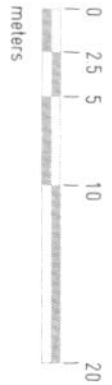
0
2.5
5
10
20
meters

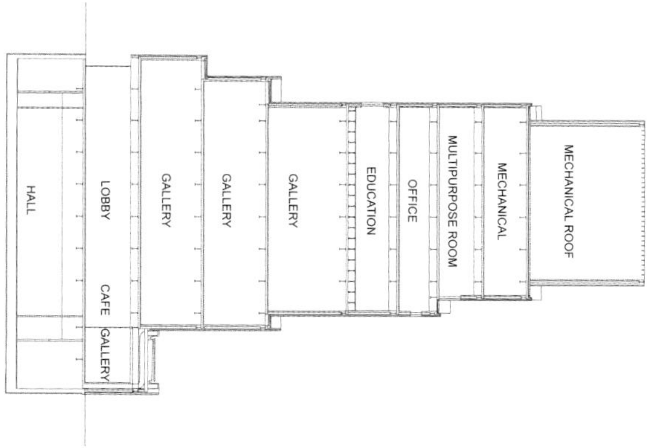
HALL
LOBBY
CAFE
GALLERY
GALLERY
GALLERY
GALLERY
EDUCATION
OFFICE
MULTIPURPOSE ROOM
MECHANICAL
MECHANICAL ROOF

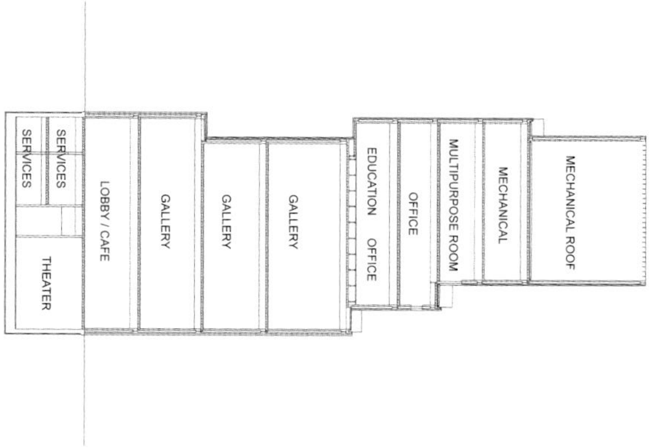
SERVICES
SERVICES
THEATER
LOBBY / CAFE
GALLERY
GALLERY
GALLERY
EDUCATION
OFFICE
OFFICE
MULTIPURPOSE ROOM
MECHANICAL
MECHANICAL ROOF

Sections

Models of the New Museum
Photo: Dean Kaufman

0 2.5 5   10   20
meters

0   2.5   5   10   20
meters

Did you at any point envisage a reading of your proposal in monumental terms, given its closeness to American Minimalist formalism?

Somehow our design feels more monumental in the models. As a building we tried to make it fit with the place, and we never thought of its roots in particular traditions.

In a museum the light is obviously very important. To what extent has the proposed treatment affected the form of the building?

The overall shape of the building might be understood as a balance between the site, the New York City building codes, and the desire to have open skylights and terraces.

The New Museum is also exceptional in its use of materials and textures. What is the functional aspect of these elements?

The texture and finish of the expanded metal are really important for the building's relationship to Bowery. We thought that it would be a good fit to the atmosphere with its depth and the industrial feeling.

What particular features of the proposed circulation scheme should we focus on?

Though it is easy to see, the circulation makes the space. The core is always in the same place while the boxes shift in relation to it, making each gallery floor different. In one instance, there are two galleries in one box divided by the core; in another, there is a corridor and a very big gallery.

And the museological program: to what extent has it determined the project?

The program determined the whole design. It is the program stacked up in the simplest terms. There were many discussions between the museum and us to fit it all together, but each decision is a part of the program.

The importance of context has become a commonplace in architectural thinking in recent decades. In this light, what are the conceptual elements — of style, of scale, for example — that have been present in the genesis of the project? What was the biggest challenge in your building for the first time in a city like New York?

Structure of analysis
and distribution
of axial forces

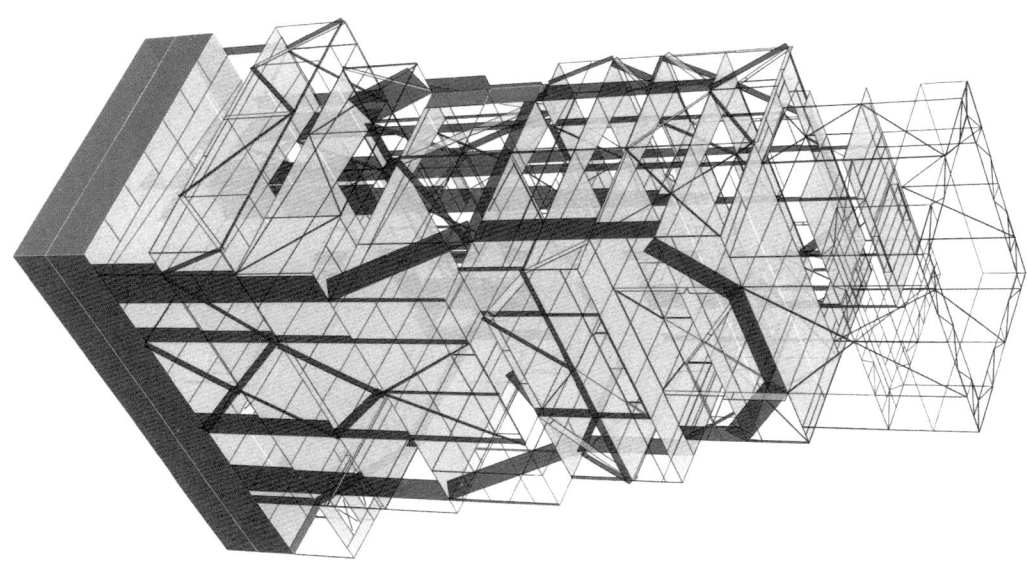

Building under construction
Photos: Dean Kaufman

Maybe more than the actual building, the institution fits well on the Bowery. We understood the New Museum and the Bowery at the same moment, and these came together to form our design. In some way the feeling in the building is under way and ongoing like the institution. The building was conceived as a bit rough, like the Bowery, but the Bowery neighborhood is getting so nice now.

In view of your intense activity in the field of museum architecture, which elements not previously present in your work should we look for in the project for the New Museum?

It is very tall.

Until very recently, the museum was regarded as a space for reflection and contemplation, the locus of aesthetic experience — with all of the mystical resonances that might be ascribed to it. What is your viewpoint now that it forms part of a dynamic of consumption which the architecture must obviously take into consideration?

We cannot deny this consumption, but we don't yet know what it means for us.

The context has a (local) spatial dimension, but it also has another cultural character. To what extent is the background of two Japanese architects visible in your first project for New York?

We know that we have something Japanese, but we ourselves do not yet have the distance to reach conclusions about it.

PHOTOGRAPHIC ESSAY

Iwan Baan

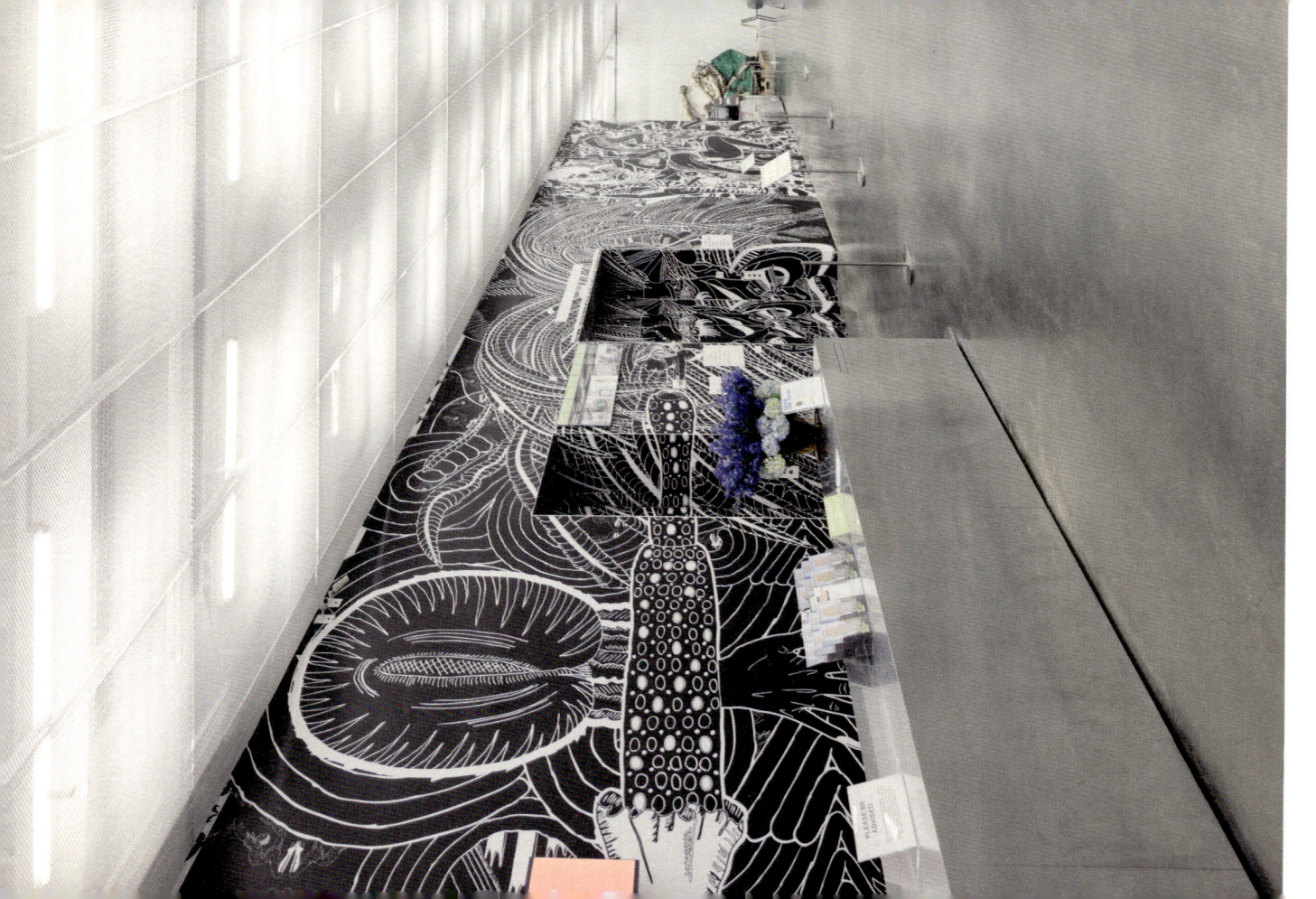

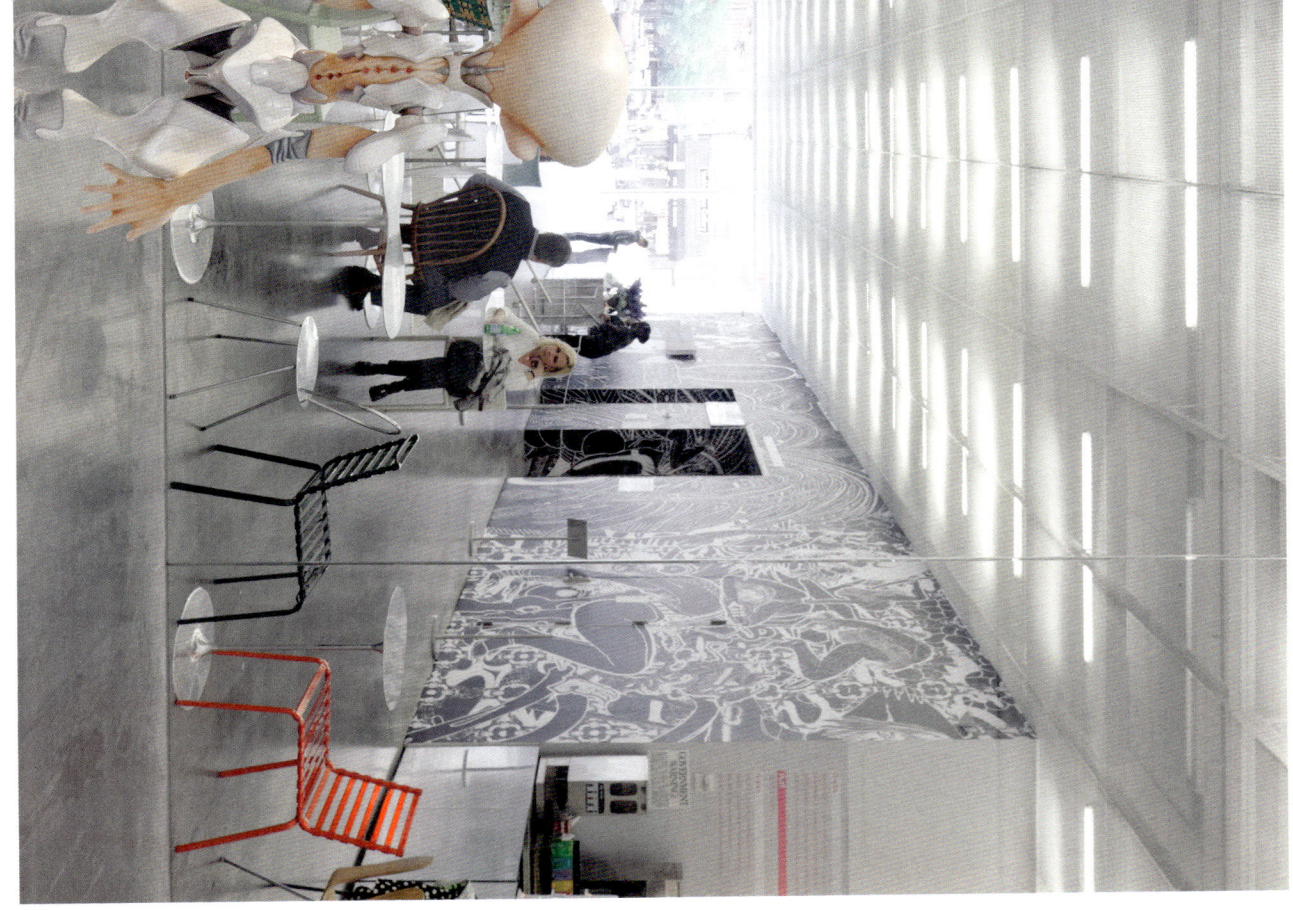

49

The New Museum of Contemporary Art is an urban infill in Downtown Manhattan. Given such a dense urban setting, stacking museum spaces might have easily led to an introverted mass. But by shifting the volumes in relation to each other, the building was opened up and the museum started to interact with its surroundings. The shifting allows for skylights and terraces while maximizing wall space and keeping within the zoned building envelope. As the relation between core and envelope varies, different lighting conditions and proportions arise.

At the inception of the project, the setbacks required by the New York City zoning regulations were a given parameter. But instead of simply allowing the zoning to make the shape of the building, its potential was of interest. Setbacks could be interactive zones. While setbacks address mass and scale, they also address how people can interact with the building and its surroundings. A setback skylight allows one to see the sky or time of day. A setback terrace allows one to stand outside and see the building up close while looking out over the neighborhood and larger city landscape. A person can leave the building and then see the setbacks from the street. This reverse perspective and memory could allow a heightened understanding of how one moved through the building. It may also allow an understanding of an individual's body scale in relation to the collective neighborhood scale. It could be an atmospheric and cognitive interaction.

People's interaction can give much life to a building. Since the New Museum is a cultural group with a strong historical connection to the neighborhood, we hope the building can become an open framework for its culture to thrive and grow with its surroundings. The Bowery has seen many changes over the decades. If people can find potential in the building, perhaps it will evolve with the neighborhood and stay relevant to changes yet to come. The simple massing and programming of the boxes are thought as in containers that can accommodate this energy. The art inside or outside can use this energy to freely continue the New Museum's relationship with the city.

The notion of definition is also important to the building. At first, the form was imagined as precisely defined boxes. But then we began to realize the roughness of the Bowery and its vibrant history. We slowly changed our concept to accept a certain un-definition and variation. The facade rendering became industrial mesh that gives depth and scale to the large surface areas. The overlapping mesh allows each panel to seamlessly integrate into the next, giving an overall monolithic appearance. The undulating surface of the mesh also gives a fuzziness that reflects all the colors and angles of the sky and cityscape. The building becomes slightly undefined as it takes on more of its surroundings. By doing so, it is open to interpretation. From far away, the museum looks soft in the landscape. From up close, its mesh diamonds look defined and rough like its neighborhood. The walk from far to close can show anything in between.

The New Museum has been open for a few years now. We have watched how the institution and neighborhood have evolved. We hope that this dynamic interaction will continue and that the building will allow its unimpeded growth for many decades to come.

Toshihiro Oki-SANAA

Project
New Museum of Contemporary Art, New York
Address
235 Bowery, New York, New York 10002
Architects
Kazuyo Sejima + Ryue Nishizawa / SANAA
Project Architects
Kazuyo Sejima, Ryue Nishizawa
Project Team
Florian Idenburg, Toshihiro Oki, Jonas Elding,
Koji Yoshida, Hiroaki Katagiri, Javier Haddad, Erika Hidaka
Associate Architects
Gensler, New York
Madeline Burke-Vigeland, Principal
Project Team
William Rice, Karen Pedrazzi, Kristian Gregerson, John Chow, Will Rohde, Sohee
Moon, Christopher Duisberg, Edgar Papazian
Project Management
Plaza Construction Corporation, New York
Planning
Competition: 2002
Construction commenced: November 2005
Building completed: October 2007
Opening: December 1, 2007
Surface area
Overall surface area: 5,450 square meters
Building contractor
Sciame, New York
Budget
$50 million
Financing
The New Museum architectural initiative is the centerpiece of a $64-million capital
project that included construction of the new building, expansion of the Museum's
endowment, and other costs related to planned growth, financed entirely by a fund-
raising campaign and the sale of the Museum's previous site on Broadway in SoHo.

Program

The new New Museum consists of eight floors above grade and two floors below, totaling nearly 5,000 square meters. The ground floor houses the Lobby, the Café, the New Museum Store, and the open loading corridor. The building has four public galleries — the Lobby Gallery located on the ground floor and three full-floor, column-free exhibition galleries on the building's second, third, and fourth levels. Each gallery has skylights for natural lighting combined with mixture lighting. One level below grade, the building's cellar level holds a 182-seat "white box" theater, a prefunction hall, and public restrooms, as well as mechanical areas, theater back-of-house functions, and storage. A workshop and additional storage areas are housed on the cellar mezzanine.

The Museum's Education Center occupies the fifth floor. Administrative offices are on the sixth floor, and a multipurpose event room (with adjacent pantry) occupies the seventh floor, surrounded by exterior terraces wrapping the east and south sides of the building. At 53.3 meters above street level, they offer uninterrupted views of downtown Manhattan.

Consultants

Executive Structural Engineer: Simpson Gumperts & Heger Incorporated, New York
Structural Engineer: Guy Nordenson and Associates, New York
Mechanical/HVAC Engineer; Electrical Systems; Audio/ Visual and I.T.: Arup
Facade: Simpson Gumperts & Heger Incorporated, New York
Waterproofing/Roofing: Henshell & Buccellato

Monographs

–Jacques Bosser, *Arquitectura + arquitectos contemporáneos*, Barcelona, Electa, 2009.

–Luis Fernández-Galiano, *Sanaa–Sejima & Nishizawa, 1990–2007*, Madrid, Arquitectura Viva, 2006.

–Yuko Hasegawa, *Kazuyo Sejima + Ryue Nishizawa Sanaa*, Milano, Electa, 2005.

–Antonello Marotta, *Contemporary museums*, Milano, Skira, 2010.

–Sanaa, *Océano De Aire* [Ocean of Air], SANAA, *Kazuyo Sejima, Ryue Nishizawa: 1998–2004*, El Escorial Madrid, Croquis, 2004.

–Sanaa, *Shift. Sanaa and the New Museum*, Lars Müller Publishers, 2008.

–Sanaa, and Moritz Küng, *Walter Niedermayr–Kazuyo Sejima–Ryue Nishizawa–Sanaa*, Ostfildern, Hatje Cantz Verlag, 2007.

–Kazuyo Sejima, and Ryue Nishizawa, *Sanaa Works 1995–2003*, 4th ed, Tokyo, Toto Shuppan, 2006.

–Kazuyo Sejima, Ryue Nishizawa, and Sanaa, SANAA. *Kazuyo Sejima + Ryue Nishizawa, 2004–2008. Topología Arquitectónica* [Architectural Topology], El Escorial Madrid, El Croquis, 2008.

–Ulrike J. Strathaus, *Sanaa–Sejima + Nishizawa*. Basel, Chritoph Merina Verlag, 2006.

Articles in Magazines

–Hubertus Adam, "Gestapelte boxen. SANAA: New Museum of Contemporary Art in New York," in *Archithese*, vol. 37, no. 5, 2007, pp. 76–77.

–Hubertus Adam, "Kein auratisieren: New Museum, New York City: SANAA," in *Bauwelt*, vol. 99, no. 4, 2008, pp. 14–21.

–Hubertus Adam, "New Museum of Contemporary Art," in *Detail*, vol. 48, no. 3, 2008, pp. 150.

–Hubertus Adam, "Stacked boxes of art: SANAA's New Museum in New York," in *Detail* (English ed.), no. 2, 2008, pp. 120–21.

–Miquel Adrià, "New Museum: El arte de la ingravidez," in *Arquine: Revista Internacional De Arquitectura y diseño* [International Architecture and Design Magazine], no. 43, 2008, pp. 14–15.

– Eve Blau, "Tensions in transparency: Between information and experience: The dialectical logic of SANAA's architecture," in *Harvard Design Magazine*, no. 29, 2008, pp. 29–37.

– Alessandro Cassin, "New Museum of Contemporary Art de Sejima y Nishizawa, New York," in *Arquine: Revista Internacional De Arquitectura y diseño* [International Architecture and Design Magazine], no. 35, 2006, p. 11.

– Giovanna Crespi, "Sejima + Nishizawa: SANAA: Europa e USA," in *Casabella*, vol. 70, no. 749, 2006, pp. 72–91.

– Elizabeth Donoff, "New Museum of Contemporary Art," in *Architectural Lighting*, vol. 22, no. 1, 2008, p. 25.

– Luis Fernández-Galiano, "2004 en doce edificios = 2004 in twelve buildings," in *AV Monografías = AV Monographs*, nos. 111–12, 2005, pp. 260–67.

– Luis Fernández-Galiano, "Alturas de Nueva York: De piano a SANAA, la cultura como motor urbano," in *Arquitectura Viva*, no. 115, 2007, pp. 80–83.

– Luis Fernández-Galiano, "Estrenos en Manhattan: Piano, New York Times, SANAA, New Museum," in *Arquitectura Viva*, no. 115, 2007.

– Luis Fernández-Galiano, "Inauguración en el Bowery: Sejima y Nishizawa en el New Museum," in *Arquitectura Viva*, no. 115, 2007, pp. 92–97.

– Kurt W. Forster, "The New Museum in New York: A whitewash?" in *Log*, no. 12, 2008, pp. 5–12.

– Joseph Giovannini, "Much askew about nothing: A thrilling facade makes empty promises at the new New Museum," in *I.D.*, vol. 55, no. 2, 2008, pp. 93–94, 100.

– Decio Guardigli, "Uno speccio dei tempi: New museum of contemporary art, New York," in *Arca*, no. 192, 2004, pp. 68–71.

– Barry Harbaugh, "Captain of Industry New Museum of Contemporary Art, New York," in *Metropolis*, vol. 27, no. 4, 2007, p. 46.

– Anna Holtzman, "SANAA: New museum of contemporary art, New York City," in *Architecture*, vol. 93, no. 2, 2004, p. 39.

– Florian Idenburg, "Light, space, and architecture: SANNA's [sic] architectural explorations with light interview," in *Architectural Lighting*, vol. 21, no.1, 2007, pp. 36–39.

– Florian Idenburg, "Meraviglioso e ruvido: Il New Museum" [Beautiful rough: The New Museum, New York, USA], in *Domus*, no. 909, 2007, pp. 12–21.

_Florian Idenburg, "SANAA's foreign mission," in *A + U: Architecture and Urbanism*, vol. 2, no. 449, 2008, pp. 122–27.

_Justin Korhammer, "Ondoorgroundelijk verlicht. New Museum in New York (USA) door Kazuyo Sejima & Ryue Nishizawa/SANAA," in *Architect* [Netherlands], vol. 39, no. 1, 2008, pp. 64–69.

_Rick Moody, "Arcobaleni all'inferno: Note sul New Museum" [Rainbows in hell: Notes on the New Museum], in *Abitare*, no. 480, 2008, pp. 114–21.

_"Museo de Arte Contemporáneo de Nueva York i.e. New Museum, New York: Kazuyo Sejima, Ryue Nishizawa, arquitectos, 2003–2007," in *Arkinka*, vol. 12, no. 155, 2008, pp. 56–69.

_"Museum in New York," in *Detail* (English ed.), no. 6, 2008, pp. 640–44, 689.

_"Museum in New York," in *Detail*, vol. 48, no. 10, 2008, pp. 1124–28, 1234.

_Philip Nobel, "Good box work: SANAA's New Museum makes compelling use of an elemental form," in *Metropolis*, vol. 27, no. 6, 2008, pp. 54, 56, 58.

_Joan Ockman, "Kazuyo Sejima + Ryue Nishizawa–SANAA: New Museum of Contemporary Art, New York," in *Casabella*, vol. 72, no. 763, 2008, pp. 70–82.

_Toshihiro Oki, and Eunjong Seong, "Collaborators for the New Museum and the Toledo Museum of Art Glass Pavilion interview," in *Space*, no. 482, 2008, pp. 80–89.

_Clifford A. Pearson, "At New York's smart New Museum of Contemporary Art, Tokyo-based SANAA creates an unambiguous icon for an area in transition," in *Architectural Record*, vol. 196, no. 3, 2008, pp. 132–39.

_"Pila de arte: New Museum of Contemporary Art, Nueva York, Estados Unidos: Kazuyo Sejima + Ryue Nishizawa, arqs," in *Summa+*, no. 104, 2009, pp. 58–65.

_"SANAA: Kazuyo Sejima, Ryue Nishizawa: 2004–2008," in *Croquis*, no. 139, 2008.

_"SANAA: New Museum, New York, 2003–07," in *Lotus International*, no. 134, 2008, pp. 108–13.

_"SANAA– Sejima & Nishizawa 1990–2007," in *AV Monografías = AV Monographs*, no. 121, 2006.

_Irénée Scalbert, "With a flowering of interest in ornament, modernism is entering a late rococo phase," in *Architecture Today*, no. 186, 2008, pp. 8, 11–12.

_Kazuyo Sejima, Cristina Díaz Moreno, and Efrén García Grinda, "SANAA: Kazuyo Sejima + Ryue Nishizawa 1998–2004," in *Croquis*, nos. 121–122, 2004.

– Kazuyo Sejima, and Juan Antonio Cortés, "SANAA Kazuyo Sejima Ryue Nishzawa, 2004-2008," in *Croquis*, no. 139, 2008.

– "Kazuyo Sejima + Ryue Nishizawa/SANAA: New Museum of Contemporary Art New York," in *Arquine. Revista Internacional De Arquitectura y diseño* [International Architecture and Design Magazine], no. 39, 2007, pp. 60-63.

– "Kazuyo Sejima + Ryue Nishizawa-SANAA: New Museum of Contemporary Art, New York, U.S.A.," in *GA Document*, no. 91, 2006, pp. 32-35.

– "Kazuyo Sejima + Ryue Nishizawa, SANAA: New Museum of Contemporary Art, U.S.A. 2003-07," in *GA Japan. Environmental Design*, no. 90, 2008, pp. 8-29.

– "Sejima+Nishizawa / SANAA: New Museum of Contemporary Art, New York, New York, U.S.A.," in *GA Document*, no. 100, 2007, pp. 92-107.

– Peter Stegner, "Museumsstapel: Das neue museum of contemporary art in Soho," in *Baumeister*, vol. 101, no. 4, 2004, p. 9.

– Carlotta Tonon, "Kazuyo Sejima + Ryue Nishizawa-SANAA: Esile come un fiore, sottile come uno specchio," in *Casabella*, vol 73, no. 784, 2009, pp. 62-69.

– Michael Webb, "Boxing clever: Museum, New York, USA," in *Architectural Review*, vol. 223, no. 1334, 2008, pp. 52-59.